Reflections

A POETIC MEMOIR

Elaine Wiley

Reflections: A Poetic Memoir
Copyright © 2023 by **Elaine Wiley**

ISBN:

Paperback: 978-1-959151-64-7

e-book: 978-1-959151-65-4

The Reading Glass Books
1-888-420-3050
www.readingglassbooks.com
production@readingglassbooks.com

Table of Contents

Introduction

"Reflections"
A Poetic Memoir

*T*hese are my collection of poems; many of which were written a few decades ago, but only recently published. Unfortunately, I did not record the date of many of the originals, but nevertheless, the point remains the same. Some of my poems were dedicated to my loved ones (children in particular) and two of my brothers, Eric and Bobby! Many of my writings were a result of my thoughts and feelings during those times. There were many dark days for me as a young woman in my twenties and even thereafter. I found some sort of relief by writing about my feelings in poetic form. It was sort of taboo to talk about certain things" back in the day," in my community, and with family members. If you expressed feelings of agitation or mistreatment by others, you were looked upon as having the problem and no one else; at least in my case. So the only thing left for me to do was hash it out of my mind, into my hand with my pen, and onto the paper.

My four recent poems are spiritual as God is my reason for being on this earth and he has kept me together when man didn't. I know he

looks over me because when I had/have no one to talk to and comfort me I go to the rock and he is there. I would sometimes feel defeated because I didn't have that earthly, physical person to talk to about my personal battles of acceptance. But somehow he allows me to weep and get back up and stand strong. I do pray that one day I will truly be accepted and respected by everyone I meet.

By Elaine Wiley

A Beautiful Girl Gets a Glare

As I look around you people stare
I say to myself: "Oh why oh why is there a stare?"
A beautiful girl gets a glare
A look of uniqueness will even get a stare
But a beautiful girl gets a glare
A misgiving of Mother Nature will even get a stare
But a beautiful girl gets a glare
As she sits in church coloring her pictures- there is a man,
There is a stare
He knows no better, because a beautiful girl gets a glare
She plays outside – enjoying the sun's glare
As people walk by there is a stare
I say to myself: "They know no better, because
a beautiful girl gets a glare!"

A Queen/The Black Woman

Accepting oneself; that brown beautiful
woman with so much potential
Loving herself unconditionally,
Seeing beauty in herself even when others don't see it
In her eyes, she's a queen who can conquer the world
with her intellect, love, caring ways and beauty
She is without a doubt, a force of nature to be reckoned with
She takes the world by storm, carrying it on her back
The provider, caretaker, disciplinarian, the
peacemaker, Yes! The Black Woman
She knows if she can perceive what she wants, she can achieve it
She walks with pride and sophistication
She knows that there's no denying her
knowledge of life and experiences
This makes her a queen who can reach out
and touch others in many ways
Her struggles allowed for growth and strength that
permeates through her body, and out of it

To help others; seeing, knowing, the precise things
that could have kept her in bondage
Allowed her to grow, glow and be of service to
the human race. A Queen indeed!

February 19, 2021

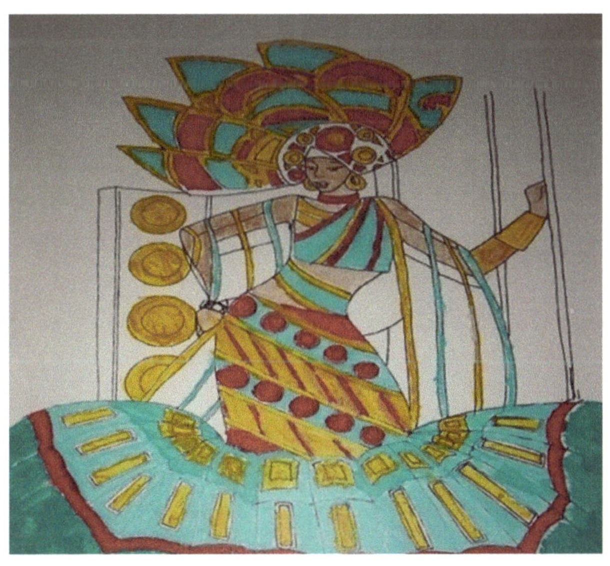

"All Up in the Cut"

We talk and reminisce about pass experiences, the
good and the bad, while "all up in the cut"

You holding me and I'm holding you, never wanting
to let go of each other, while "all up in the cut"

Caressing each other, enjoying the feelings we
both get, while "all up in the cut"

Both realizing that we are not only physically drawn to each other,
but emotionally and mentally as well, while "all up in the cut"

Sharing ideas of possibilities, excited about what
could be, while "all up in the cut"

Complimenting and accepting each other's characteristics,
both physical and mental, while "all up in the cut"

Knowing each other's quirks, humor, hick ups, and
limitations, all while "all up in the cut

*Apologizing for any wrongdoings, by one or both of us, and
expressing it through a warm embrace, while "all up in the cut"
Never wanting to let go as we gaze into each other's eyes, with
looks of admiration for each other, while "all up in the cut"*

*Never wanting to let go as we gaze into each other's eyes, with
looks of admiration for each other, while "all up in the cut"*

*Forgetting our age and fully engaging in the romanticism
of a young love, while "all up in the cut"*

*Realizing, with each moment, how much we really love and appreciate
each other, and never wanting to let go as we lay, "All up in the cut"*

June 28, 2022

"Baby Girl"

"Baby Girl"—You would say upon seeing mom

She'd look at you and smile as if she knew she'd be alright
Allowing her to see that she wasn't alone in her journey or plight
And that you, her son Bobby would always be by her side
No matter what time or place, to guide
Your never ending bond only increased over time
Never hesitating to respond at the drop of a dime
Taking care of her through trials and tribulations
Seeking the best care for her, regardless of relocations
Never thinking about your own circumstances,
Only your mom –"Baby Girl"

Keeping the family informed of her bouts,
As she endured this new way of living throughout
Trapped in her body, unable to speak,
Allowed for uneasiness, uncertainty, but kisses on the cheek,
For your –"Baby Girl"

Knowing who she was, created irritability,
It was like someone else had taken control and she could no longer be
The utter of one word (money) and another word
(Betty) used to explain what she was trying to say,
Only lead to confusion and agitation with everyone who came her way
Yes- Your Baby Girl

Making sure she had the utmost comfort and attention to her needs
You allowed the professionals to care for her through your lead
Complimenting the staff for their genuine concern and attention
provided them with hope, gratitude and admiration to mention
Inspiring them to keep up the good work with your mom, "Baby Girl"

You showed her that she had a son of
unconditional love and admiration
You were her rock, and she was your mom, "Baby Girl!"

Dedicated to my brother, Bobby
for his/our mother "Baby Girl!"
8/31/2022

Basketball

You hoop that ball into the net
And move around until you get set
Front and back and side to side
Like a real star you even glide
You block and pass and do your thing
Next you hoop that ball right in the ring
Now you've scored you feel "fly"
The game must go on you can't deny

You run and jump and stop that ball
The other team hopes for a foul call
Now you're excited you can't wait
To take the game to another "state"
You look around to find your man
6Ft.4, that's him with a tan
You pass the ball he receives
He slam dunks, and now he leaves
Now you set up for another day
The game must go on ending your way

Dedicated to my son, "Dre"
October 1, 2008

Dancers

They sway, they tap, they stretch
How remarkable are they
They swing they bend, they lean
How remarkable are they
They jump, they glide, they step
How remarkable are they
From jazz to rhythmic soul
They dance
Remarkable Dancers

"Employability Factor"

Your age, your race, your gender, your
looks, your school, your religion
Where does it end?
You seek employment-yet there's deterrence, we have no openings
You have education, talent, intelligence, adaptability, skills
Yet you're just another needle in a haystack
You're not bilingual, but you know more than many who are
You are disregarded
What is this economy coming to?
Is it the need to keep certain people of particular
characteristics in the forefront?
Ignoring those who have qualities complimentary to the employer
When does it end?
When will those people open their eyes and see what really matters?

This poem was written some decades ago while
experiencing challenges in the work arena.

Entrapment

You say to yourself I'm finished enough is enough
      You still carry on that "finished thing"
Sometimes it's need and sometimes it's not
      It's sometimes the forceful nature of another
To refuse to let go of something never "legally" claimed
      You push it away but it says please stay
It still finds a way back another day
      You say to yourself "I'm tired of this thing"
You give it a go because of the offspring
      There's no connection it does not work
You say to yourself "I knew it wasn't so
      You've tried, tried, tried
Still no connection of that finished thing
      It's time to move on and be your own thing

Yet still it refuses-There's an offspring
      You are entrapped

Escape!

The stroke of a pen, so pleasant, so beautiful
You use it to encounter another place;
somewhere you've never gone before
You're in a dream world, yet it is reality based
Your problems become minute with each stroke

Analogous to the alcoholic; who drinks to dissolve his problems
When the intoxication wears off, the issues are still prevalent
He feels good; he has forgotten the unpleasantries of his life for a while

Analogous to the overeater; who seeks comfort through foods
The more she eats the better she feels
She has become focused on foods, and less focused on her problems

Analogous to the physical trainer; who works out day and
night to stay fit, release tension, prevent aggression
Doing what it takes to alleviate his innermost problems
Although after the workout, the problem still persists
He has found a way to deal with it even if only for a few hours

He has escaped!

Fathers and Daughters

Fathers —Their special bond, like glue, sticking close to their daughters
    Their love is ever so true

Watching them grow, like seeds to a flower, it blooms
That beautiful baby girl will one day have a groom

Because of that seed you planted in her
She will always remember to say hello and thank you sir

Respecting herself and demanding the same
Will allow her to reminiscence on that which she came

Acknowledging and admiring her accomplishment
Gives her confidence to succeed beyond astonishment

That bubbly little girl dressed in pink
Can now dance with her father and think

My dad loves me there's no denying
I will always honor him and never stop trying

To do my best in life and make him proud
That his little girl has soared beyond the clouds

(2014)

Four Men of Despair

They have been served an injustice
They need not speak-It is written on their faces
They have been wronged
It is the look of despair, disbelief, disappointment, and hopelessness
They know not where they're headed, but hope
it's not worse than where they've been
Their experience has not been pleasant
It has warranted them the mistrusting of the overseer
As you look through the glasses of four victims,
it is clear, justice has not been served
His vision remains clear, and he will not rest until
justice prevails over the sadness he feels
But there is still hope for tomorrow-for all of them
Tomorrow has to be a brighter day

"Hair Apparel"

Try it on
You like it
Look in the mirror
It's a good fit
Take it home
Put it on your dome
You like it You wear it
Looks good on you
It's a perfect fit
Let it lay
Put it on another day
Looks different on you
Not as good
Take it off like you should
Store it away
Go shopping
Find another one that's popping
Try it on you like it
Look in the mirror it's a good fit
Like "Déjà Vu"
It goes home with you

"*Imagine*"

Imagine you are in a place of humbleness; tranquility
Imagine you are ever so beautiful; glowing eyes and hair: flawless skin
Imagine your body perfectly proportioned:
as you walk everyone takes notice
Imagine you are one of many physically beautiful people
Imagine that beauty transcending through your personality
Imagine – That distinguishing you from all the
other beautiful people in the world

Fast forward decades later:
Imagine what really counts in life, love, happiness, health,
family, and of course, spirituality. Imagine putting all those
things above physical beauty and seeing life from a whole new
perspective. Just imagine where life could take us! Imagine

Kelly

Gone but never forgotten! Your smile lights up any room. Never
loud as I know you, but your presence naturally draws attention

My young cousin, full of life, dreams, and hope for the future
Is now with God in heaven, as one of his angels,
lighting up the skies with your glow
My daughter, your second cousin, would see you now and then
She'd often say, "Mom I saw Kelly today!" As if
she was reunited with a sister every time
Blessed with a mother twice and a daughter once

You are loved beyond measure
Just like silver and gold you're our real treasure
Love has no boundaries; neither does our love for you
Your beautiful smile and beautiful spirit will always remain true
God has placed you amongst his angels
So rest in peace, and away from the earthly mangels

Love you always,
Cousin Elaine

Loneliness

You seek the companion of another, but it seems you're still alone
You look for that male strength to support you, you're still all alone
You look for that motherly bond, It has
been broken, but slowly mending
You still feel alone
Your brother-sister bond is prevalent, but you're still alone
A close relative who was like a sister, becomes distant
Now you're alone
You go out your way to keep friends, yet you're all alone
You're an only child of your dad, he doesn't really know you
Still you're very much alone

Written three decades ago!

Magnetic Attraction/Love

Visiting your place for meetings you would often stare
As to wonder what a woman like me was all about
Especially one in particular-A Birthday Dinner for our business leader
You watched me as I walked back and forth across the room
Another member watched you watching me
Hilarious, but true
It was as though nothing or no one else mattered
We all talked, ate, and sipped apple cider
So thirst quenching and good
But so was your admiration for me, staring so intensely
Me never feeling uncomfortable, but flattered
as you took notice of my assets
Feeling wonderfully adored by someone I only knew a few weeks
As the meetings continued, so did our interests in each other
Not only that physical attraction, but mental/
emotional attraction as well
Conversations of similar view points, spirituality, love,
communication, as well as physical attraction-Magnetic
Never thinking, knowing, feeling this would happen

But just allowing nature to take its course as we embrace on our
journey of discovering each other, unveiling self discovery
Taking inventory of this new profound love that has
blossomed into such a relationship-never imagined
No holding back, no precautions, no interference
For what God has bought together
No monetary influence-Just pure unsaturated, undeniable, love
Respecting that other person and receiving it in return
Acknowledging the good and bad, but complementing the good
Keeping your spirits high as you keep mines
Never forsaking the other person, realizing his importance
Comforting each other, as that necessary ingredient
of mental and physical wellness
How wonderful is it to find that person who makes
you laugh and cry, interchangeably, and you he
No doubt about it, love has found its way to
my heart, to your heart, to our hearts
No denying it, just allowing love to flow
Your warm embrace brings comfort, joy, and
security I've never known before
Our attraction for one another-without a doubt-Magnetic!

September 3, 2021

Man/Not

Man - an adult human being of the male species
Woman-an adult human being of the female species

Do not refer to me as "man" when I am your daughter
Do not refer to me as "man" when I am your sister
Do not refer to me as "man" when I am your mother
Do not refer to me as "man" when I am your wife/partner
Do not refer to me as "man" when I am your female friend

A man I am not
A man I am not
A woman I am
A woman I am

My Centerpiece

A figure I see as my eyes are closed
Red-outlined in turquoise
Shaped like a snowman
Asking myself-What does it mean?
Closing my eyes over and over again to see the figure
To make sense of it
The color remaining the same
The figure remaining the same
What does it mean?
Turquoise-My favorite color
Jesus-My all in all
Red represents the blood of Jesus
My favorite color/Turquoise
Surrounding the red figure/Jesus Christ
I am Turquoise
Red Is Jesus
Jesus is my centerpiece

May 23, 2017

My Face

As I look in the mirror
I see my face
Reflection of my Mom
Father
Grandma
Looking back at me

Like a cut-out cardboard
Chiseled like pie
It's my mom

Beaming eyes and
Arched eyebrows
Look of absolute
It's my Dad's

Patches of moles
One big one on right side
It's my grandmas

Face of many characteristics
Happy/sad
Mean/angry
Pretty/ugly
Female/male

Peculiar to others

It's Jamaican
Haitian
African

Indeed
African American
My face

My Testimony

My testimony is not some drastic event that
occurred and made me change to God's way
It's not telling other's stories or events of tragedy to triumph
My testimony is the "fact" that God is always there for me
Through sickness and health
Through ups and downs
Those times of drastic bodily changes-aches
and pains, emotional turmoil, stress
"You" (God) pulled me together
Put weight back on my bones
Put confidence back in my head
Put energy back in my body
Put spirit back in my soul
"You" allowed me to see that there is light at the end of the tunnel
No matter what the issues were, you were there
Your protection of my family, their health, their safety
In the midst of unjust and evil in the world, it's unparalleled
But most of all, you have allowed me to see another day.

10/30/2016

One Life To Live

You only get one life to live
Do the things you want
So there's no regret to haunt
Stop being a victim to the world
And show that you're a conqueror and a pearl
Cause you only got one life to live

Help others when you can
It doesn't matter who's the man
Show appreciation for your help
And remember never to skelp
Cause you only got one life to live

Always give thanks to the entity above
It's because of him that you show love
It's that force that keeps us together
And it never matters what the weather
Cause you only got one life to live

So be the best you can
And stay above the sand
Make it your best
And don't forget the rest
Cause you only got one life to live

Hold your head up high
And let your thoughts soar through the skies
You only got one life to live

Perseverance

You raise your hand to respond
Yet you're ignored
You're told you're wrong, your answer is stupid
Yet, you continue to pursue knowledge
You're looked at as peculiar
Yet you continue to be you
You're disliked, you don't fit in
Yet you seek personal satisfaction
You're stared at, wondering what it could be
You deserve so much attention
Without a blink of an eye, no word said
Are you a star and don't know it
Are you a powerful force of nature, which magnetizes people?
They cannot control their focus
Whatever the energies, negative or positive
You continue to persevere

Written some decades ago

Rejection

Not accepted by family/others
People-saying, thinking, acting, reacting
You're not important/ you're beneath them
From youth /being ridiculed by others
Words that may or may not symbolize you
Family/speaking to you with disrespect
You respond/perhaps negatively
You become the problem/another reason to distance themselves
Deep in inside you know it is beyond personality
Every human being has personality issues
But everyone is not rejected by family/friends
Only a select few
Rejection/ That underlying demon that allows
for unacceptability/based on physicality
You don't meet expectations or qualifications to be accepted

June 17, 2017

Respect/What does it mean?

You may not know me, like me, adore me
Does that mean you disrespect, antagonize, ignore me

You may not know me, like me, adore me
Does that mean you look with disgust, talk about me, laugh at me
You may not know me, like me, adore me
Does that mean you condescend, degrade, and disassociate me?

You may not know me, like me, adore me
Does this mean you insult, ridicule, compare me?

You may not know me, like me, adore me
Does this mean we cannot coexist in this world with
respect, humility, consideration, humanity?
Respect-What does it mean?

September 8, 2016

She Swings

She swings as high as the bushes
Up and away she goes
Back and forth, wiggling her little toes
Smiling and hollering with so much joy
Not wanting to stop
Like playing with a favorite toy
She swings and swings
It's thirty minutes or more
She doesn't mind it's not a bore
A push from a girl gives her more of a swing
She swings a little more
And gets down off that thing

October 1, 2008

Sleepless Nights

You wake up; it's 3:00 in the morning
    You release your urine, another sleepless night
Thoughts running wild, why can't I sleep?
    Sighing, tossing, turning, listening to music
Thinking you're blessed and cursed at the same time
    Your beautiful offsprings- happy, healthy, wise
Your appearance – not accepted by others; family, friends, outsiders
    Criticized, disrespected, ignored; a misfit of society
Yet you remain strong
    As real as you are you put on a nice, optimistic face
Deep inside you hurt and long for that acceptability
from others as well as yourself
    You look in the mirror and question
God-Why me? I'm a good person
Yet society doesn't care how good you are if you don't look the part
    You are a nobody
You're intelligence, talents, and niceness accounts for nothing
    You are just a squirrel trying to get a nut
You take inventory of your life, your mistakes and triumphs
    You say to yourself, "I'm singled out more"
It's my physicality and not my personality that's attacked
Yet you are one in the same

*Any confrontations resulting from mistreatments appears to
be your problem with others and not others with you
        You just "ball up" and wish you could
feel better and return to sleep
This thought process repeats itself, another sleepless night*

2005

Thank You God For The Sunlight

As I awaken and stand at my balcony's window,
your sunlight is shining bright on me

A blast of vitamin D through the warm window
pain, as your sunlight is shining bright on me

Issues of the world become temporarily obsolete,
as your sunlight shines bright on me

No taking for granted God's creation, that which all plants
and animals grow, the sunlight that shines bright on me

Thank you God for the sun, your light is shining bright on me

It warms my body and enlightens my mind,
to feel the sun shining bright on me

*It gives me hope for a better day, because
your sun is shining bright on me*

*Thank you, God for giving me the sun, representing your
warmth, nurture, and everlasting love, to shine on me.*

March 9, 2021

The Clock Ticks

The sounds of snoring in the middle of the night
As the clock ticks
There is tossing and turning and stretching and coughing
Still the clock ticks
The water drips from the faucet, plop, plop, plop
The clock continues to tick
There is the calmness of night-Even At 4:12 in the morning,
As there is the sound of tick tick
Your cover comes off; you pull it back over you
Yet your hear the sound of tick tick
You're up at night and you hear an ambulance siren
But you still hear the clock ticking
The refrigerator cuts off to regenerate-you
still hear the clock going tick tick

As babies are born
As people are procreating
As people are passing on
The clock continues to tick!

The Straw That Broke the Camel's Back/Dedicated to Eric and DeeDee

Like" Bonnie and Clyde" Always together through thick and thin
 When "K" fought, Bonnie jumped in
They knew the streets like the back of their hand
Walking, talking, seeing, knowing people
 Yes, many, many fans
Like celebrities often greeted, smiled at, respected
 But young, carefree, and much to be corrected
The ins and outs of experimentation
 Allowed for problems and rocky relations
Experiences with the unjust/alcohol and drugs/whether hot or cold
 Only led to destruction of mind, body, and soul
Running from the law, leaping from above
 Almost losing your life/perhaps never again able to love

A broken ankle you endured
    Yes, survival instincts loudly roared
Learning from your mistakes and moving forward
    Allowed for better things to head towards
There's no more "Bonnie and Clyde"
    But Mr. and Mrs. for the long ride
A positive force in life, you have become
    Helping others see, they too can overcome

June 13, 2011
Sis (Elaine)

The Wake up Call

(Dedicated to my brother Bobby)

You're working with the landlord on a house
Assisting him with aluminum siding
Looking at the chimney coming down towards you
Running and tripping over bushes to get out of harm's way
The chimney falling on your head, causing unconsciousness
Causing brain swelling, causing a skull fracture
You lay comatose for two months, as per doctor's orders
You awaken, your mind returning to your childhood
Talking as if you're down south with family there
Each day your memory coming closer to the present
You finally get in touch with reality, recognizing family and friends
You're truly delighted
Your mother, girlfriend, and I, not so
delighted, you've obtained a bed sore
We confront your caregivers, their job, not effective
We cleanse and comfort you, you're delighted
We leave and return another day, the sore barely there
Our talk to the caregivers, an effective process

Your personality soon becoming apparent to your caregivers
"Fussing" about things you need, and saying things like
"my mouth is dry, give me something to drink"
The staff, really liking you and informing us of your "bouts" with them
You, keeping them on their toes

Now you must start again, you have been given a second chance
You're future becoming brighter than you've ever known
No longer are you "running the streets" hanging out
No longer are you drinking "King Cobra" and smoking marijuana
No longer are you getting into trouble with friends
You are now more positive, thinking about your future,
Obtaining your high school diploma through a home course
Going to church
Your future looks brighter!
You have truly awakened!

October 1, 2008

The Woman Within

I am she and she is me

Looking- *As I look in the mirror, I see you, and say, I look like mom*

Talking- *I converse with a friend as if she was still here, giving him a glimpse of your personality, he says, she's the woman within*

Thinking- *I think about our talks, actions, determination, and energy; similar*

Bearing- *You bear one girl and the rest boys, I-a duplication of this process*

Caring- *Your family; sisters, brothers, children of great importance/my view is family first*

Knowing- *You always knew how to keep your family afloat and provide guidance, even if they didn't adhere to it*

Living- *You lived life to fullest until you could no longer; a superb cook, trips, beaches, parties, card games, soft ball, and the list goes on*

Achieving- *You've obtained the honor of queen, not only because of your position in the family, but because of what you've endured as a young girl, woman, and mom, until your demise*

You are/were truly a warrior without realizing it
Hoping that what I see in the mirror is a warrior as well
For you are the woman within me I

The Woman Within (2)

__Showing__ how to take care of family, house, you without saying
Never hiding behind words, expressive at all levels
__Providing__ the utmost atmosphere for your loved ones, because of your upbringing
__Giving__ unconditionally because that's your nature
Always a leader and never a follower, setting an example for others without trying
__Having__ that innate quality to conquer anything you put your mind to
__Knowing__ and experiences beyond your years, allowed for enjoyment of fruits from your labor
__Being__ stylish and photogenic without trying, even with a scarf and hair rollers, photo ready
__Instilling__ values without preaching

__Yes! The Woman Within__

Thunder In The Park

We arrive in the park
She, her son, my daughter and I
We didn't know it would be such a cloudy sky
We sat for a while
As the children played, there was just a sprinkle
So we stayed
The drops, heavier, faster, bolder
We told the children, It's time to leave
It's getting colder
We grabbed the children and started to walk
Then there's thunder's roar, not even she could talk
A streak of lightening glistened the sky
We looked with fright and the children cried
We ran for shelter in the park's bathroom
We jerked with panic
My friend, her son, my daughter and I
We huddled our children and then there was a boom
We jerked with panic

My friend, her son, my daughter and I
The children looked and loudly cried
It stopped a minute, we also paused
Then it came crashing down, like a locomotive train
What has the sky caused?
We huddled and prayed, my friend and I
That we would be safe and not die
Then there's another glistening of the sky
We could see it through the ceiling
The glasslike structure was too revealing
We talked to the children and continued to pray
Hoping this storm would go away
As we listened, the loud booms died down
The glistening light stopped
We told the children, let's make a run for the car, go
We all ran, my sandal slipped in the puddle
I put it on and dashed to the car
We all got in
As I drove, my friend and I said, I'll never
go to the park on a cloudy day again!

2005

Turmoil

You argue and fight to no end
  I wonder what could cause such a wind
Like a hurricane coming through a city with destruction
  The two of you behave like former inmates of corruption
The substances you inhale into your system
  Throws your mind into a frenzy, completely off rhythm
It causes you to act out violently, without a care
  To even kill because of a dare
Its poison to your body and mind, without a doubt
  You react to your oppressor volatile, with a quarrel and shout
The family dynamics have been interrupted
  By your temper, attitude, and alcohol- so abrupt
Your age should matter when choosing to behave
  In such a way that causes an up and down wave
You play the blame game, and verbally attack others

Not realizing that your relationship should be like brothers
In your eyes you are under attack and the victim
But you cannot change until you admit
The problem is you and not the system

Oct. 13, 2016

Unconditional Love

Don't love me or like me because I'm there for you
Don't love me or like me because I listened
to you when no one else would
Don't love me or like me because I was your only outlet
Don't love me or like me because I look a particular way today
Don't love me or like me because you need something today or tomorrow
Don't love me or like me because I had children
and then became important

When you love or like me because of what I can do for you or how I
look today, then how true is the love? Is it unconditional? I think not!
Conditional love has boundaries
Unconditional love knows no boundaries
It accepts one as is
No words needed or activities to perform
It is you and only you that matters-Truly Unconditional

"Who Are You?"

Are you the one who sits and waits for the Q?
Or are you the one who takes the initiative of the crew?
Are you the one who diverts his view; sway?
Or are you the one who says I'll do it my way?
Are you the one who leaves when the going gets tough?
Or are you the one who deals with the challenge, no matter how rough?
Are you the one who lets others determine your worth?
Or are you the one who strives to do good on earth?

Who Are You?

The White Light/God/Jesus

As I praise your name and my eyes are closed
I see a light, white, candle-like
Symbolizing-You are the light of my life
> *The direction of my pathways*
> *The reminder of my never ending love for you*
You guide me
You protect me
You deliver me
You keep me moving forward
May that light forever burn in my heart/my mind/my body and soul
Yes-The White Light

February 7, 2017